Neon Soundscapes

A History of 12th Planet

Leila Yamamoto

ISBN: 9781779693426
Imprint: Press for Play Books
Copyright © 2024 Leila Yamamoto.
All Rights Reserved.

Contents

Introduction: Who the Fuck Is 12th Planet?

The Godfather of American Dubstep: How 12th Planet Helped Fucking Shape the Dubstep Scene

From Drum and Bass to Dubstep: How 12th Planet Fucking Found His Sound

In order to understand how 12th Planet, the godfather of American Dubstep, found his unique sound, we must first explore his early beginnings in the world of drum and bass. John Dadzie, known by his stage name 12th Planet, initially emerged in the music scene as a Drum and Bass DJ and producer. It was through his journey in this genre that he eventually discovered and pioneered the genre of dubstep in the United States.

The Fucking LA Underground Scene: How 12th Planet Cut His Fucking Teeth in the Drum and Bass World

Born and raised in Los Angeles, 12th Planet was exposed to the vibrant underground music scene that thrived in the city. The LA drum and bass scene, in particular, captivated his attention and fueled his passion for electronic music. He immersed himself in the pulsating beats, complex rhythms, and captivating basslines that defined the genre.

Eager to make his mark, 12th Planet started DJing at local clubs, warehouse raves, and underground parties. These intimate spaces of musical expression allowed him to connect with the crowd on a deeper level. He quickly gained a reputation for his electrifying sets and his ability to energize the dance floor.

How 12th Planet Discovered Fucking Dubstep and Became a Fucking Pioneer of the Genre in the US

While fully immersed in the drum and bass scene, 12th Planet stumbled upon a revolutionary sound that would change the course of his musical journey forever – dubstep. Intrigued by its gritty basslines, half-time rhythms, and dark atmospheres, he began to explore this emerging genre.

Fueled by curiosity and an unquenchable thirst for musical experimentation, 12th Planet meticulously studied the intricacies of dubstep production. He spent countless hours dissecting tracks, analyzing sound design techniques, and honing his craft.

Through this process, 12th Planet found his own voice within the dubstep scene. He started incorporating elements of his drum and bass background into his dubstep productions, adding a unique flavor to his sound. His love for complex drum patterns and intricate basslines became his signature style, earning him recognition as a true innovator in the genre.

The Fucking Shift: How 12th Planet Blended Fucking Drum and Bass with Dubstep to Create His Fucking Unique Sound

12th Planet's transition from drum and bass to dubstep was not a simple abandonment of one genre for another. Instead, it was a transformative process that allowed him to fuse the best elements of both genres.

Drawing from his extensive knowledge of drum and bass, 12th Planet seamlessly integrated rapid-fire breaks, intricate percussion, and relentless energy into his dubstep compositions. This fusion of genres resulted in a sound that was both aggressive and captivating, pushing the boundaries of what was thought possible in the emerging realm of dubstep.

Case Studies: Early Fucking Releases That Defined 12th Planet's Fucking Entry Into Dubstep

As 12th Planet began to establish himself as a pioneer in the American dubstep scene, he released several tracks that showcased his unique sound and style. One notable example is his track "68", which blended dubstep's heavy bass drops with the frenetic energy of drum and bass. The track gained significant attention and solidified 12th Planet's reputation as a groundbreaking artist.

Another notable release was "Purple & Gold," a collaboration with dubstep heavyweight Datsik. This track highlighted 12th Planet's ability to create immersive, atmospheric dubstep while infusing elements of his drum and bass roots. It became an instant hit, propelling him even further into the limelight.

The Fucking Future of Bass Music: Will 12th Planet's Fucking Roots in Drum and Bass Continue to Influence His Fucking Music?

As 12th Planet's career continues to evolve, the influence of his drum and bass roots remains a fundamental aspect of his music. While he has become synonymous with the dubstep genre, he consistently explores new sonic territories, pulling inspiration from various genres, including drum and bass.

By blending elements from different genres, 12th Planet continuously pushes the boundaries of bass music, challenging expectations and creating a unique sonic experience for his audience. As his sound continues to evolve, it is clear that his maturation as an artist is deeply rooted in his diverse musical background.

In the coming years, we can expect 12th Planet to further expand the boundaries of bass music, incorporating elements from his drum and bass heritage and collaborating with other genre-bending artists. His relentless pursuit of sonic innovation will undoubtedly shape the future of not only dubstep but also the wider electronic music landscape.

Conclusion

In this section, we explored the journey of 12th Planet from his early days in the LA drum and bass scene to his pioneering role in the emergence of dubstep in America. We witnessed how his passion for music led him to discover and create a unique sound that blends the best aspects of drum and bass with the emerging genre of dubstep.

Through case studies and examples, we witnessed the evolution and influence of 12th Planet's sound, and how his fusion of genres continues to shape the bass music scene. We also discussed the impact of his drum and bass roots on his music, highlighting his ability to constantly push the boundaries of what is expected from a dubstep artist.

As we look to the future, it is clear that 12th Planet's legacy in shaping the dubstep genre will continue to grow. His unwavering commitment to innovation and fearless experimentation guarantees that his influence on the bass music scene will endure for years to come.

The Fucking Role of Los Angeles in the Rise of American Dubstep: 12th Planet's Fucking Contribution to the Scene

Los Angeles, the city of dreams, has played a pivotal role in the rise of American dubstep. As the home of diverse music scenes and a breeding ground for innovation, LA provided the perfect backdrop for artists like 12th Planet to make their mark and shape the dubstep movement in the United States. In this section, we will delve into the fucking importance of Los Angeles in the dubstep scene and explore 12th Planet's fucking significant contribution to its development.

Los Angeles has long been a fucking hub for music and artistic expression. The city's vibrant nightlife scene, characterized by its plethora of clubs, underground parties, and music festivals, created an ideal environment for a new genre like dubstep to thrive. As the city attracted artists and musicians from various backgrounds, it became a melting pot of creativity and cross-pollination of musical styles.

In the early 2000s, when dubstep was still in its infancy, LA became a breeding ground for dubstep pioneers like 12th Planet. He emerged as one of the key figures responsible for bringing the genre to the forefront of American electronic music. Through his relentless dedication to pushing boundaries and his unique sound, 12th Planet helped solidify LA's position as a powerhouse in the dubstep scene.

One of the fucking crucial contributions 12th Planet made to the rise of American dubstep was through his involvement in the formation of SMOG, a dubstep record label and collective based in Los Angeles. SMOG became a central platform for dubstep artists in the city, bringing together like-minded individuals and fostering a sense of community. It served as a launching pad for many emerging talents, providing them with opportunities to showcase their music and collaborate with established artists.

In addition to his role in the creation of SMOG, 12th Planet's fucking relentless touring and live performances across Los Angeles played a pivotal role in exposing the local audience to dubstep. His energetic sets and seamless transitions incorporated a wide range of subgenres, attracting both longtime electronic music fans and newcomers alike. Through his performances, 12th Planet introduced LA to the fucking mesmerizing and raw power of dubstep, garnering a dedicated following and inspiring a new generation of artists in the process.

Furthermore, 12th Planet's collaborations with other influential artists in the LA music scene, such as Skrillex and Excision, helped solidify the city's reputation as a hotbed of dubstep talent. These joint efforts not only expanded his reach but also showcased the collaborative and experimental nature of the genre. As they broke down musical boundaries and merged various styles, they paved the way for a new era of bass music that would transcend the confines of conventional electronic music.

The impact of Los Angeles on the rise of American dubstep cannot be overstated. Its vibrant music scene, coupled with its diverse and open-minded audience, created a fertile ground for the genre to flourish. 12th Planet, through his fucking innovative productions, his role in establishing SMOG, and his electrifying performances, played a significant part in shaping dubstep's trajectory in the city.

Looking ahead, the influence of Los Angeles in the dubstep scene shows no signs of waning. The city continues to produce talented artists, fostering a sense of creativity and experimentation that pushes the genre forward. As 12th Planet's fucking legacy continues to insp

ire emerging artists, we can expect to see an ongoing evolution of American dubstep, with Los Angeles at its fucking epicenter.

Case Study: The Transformation of Skrillex

An exemplary case study of the fucking impact of Los Angeles and 12th Planet's influence on the rise of American dubstep is the transformation of Skrillex. Born Sonny Moore, Skrillex originally found success as the frontman of the post-hardcore band From First to Last. However, it was his move to Los Angeles and immersion in its diverse music scene that led to his dubstep reinvention.

In LA, Skrillex was introduced to the likes of 12th Planet and other prominent dubstep artists. Inspired by their groundbreaking sound, he began experimenting with dubstep and electronic music production. Skrillex's collaboration with 12th Planet on the track "Needed Change" marked a turning point in his career, showcasing his newfound love for dubstep.

Building on this experience, Skrillex went on to release his groundbreaking EP, "Scary Monsters and Nice Sprites," which catapulted him to international fame. The EP's unique combination of aggressive basslines, melodic hooks, and intricate sound design became synonymous with the evolving American dubstep sound, with its influence spreading far beyond the confines of the genre.

Skrillex's success story serves as a testament to the fucking impact of Los Angeles and 12th Planet's contribution to the rise of American dubstep. It showcases how the city's diverse music scene and collaborative spirit can create an environment that nurtures and inspires transformational artistic journeys.

The Fucking Future of Dubstep: Will 12th Planet's Fucking Legacy Continue to Shape the Bass Fucking Music Scene?

How 12th Planet Fucking Pushed the Boundaries of Bass Music with His Fucking Signature Style

12th Planet, the Godfather of American Dubstep, is not just a pioneer in the genre; he is also known for pushing the boundaries of bass music with his unique and innovative style. Throughout his career, 12th Planet has continually challenged the norms and expectations of the genre, constantly evolving and experimenting with his sound. His distinctive signature style has left a lasting impact on bass music, inspiring countless artists and shaping the future of the genre.

Exploring New Soundscapes: The Fucking Fusion of Genres

One of the ways 12th Planet pushed the boundaries of bass music was through his fearless exploration and fusion of different genres. He seamlessly blended elements of dubstep, drum and bass, and other electronic genres to create a sound that was truly his own. By combining these diverse influences, 12th Planet introduced a fresh and exciting sonic palette to the bass music scene.

For example, in his track "Reasons," 12th Planet incorporated elements of hip-hop, infusing the heavy basslines and hard-hitting beats with rap vocals. This fusion of genres not only showcased his versatility as a producer but also broke down the traditional boundaries between different musical styles. His fearless experimentation with diverse genres opened new doors for bass music, encouraging other artists to explore unconventional combinations and push the limits of their own sound.

Innovative Sound Design: The Fucking Creation of New Textures

Another aspect of 12th Planet's signature style is his innovative sound design, which has revolutionized the way bass music is produced. He is known for his intricate and complex bass patterns, characterized by their gritty, aggressive, and razor-sharp quality. 12th Planet's commitment to pushing the boundaries of sound has led him to develop unique techniques and processes to create his distinctive bass textures.

For instance, in his track "Rasputin," 12th Planet employs intricate modulation techniques to manipulate and shape the sound of the bass. By experimenting with different types of distortion, filtering, and modulation effects, he creates a dynamic and evolving bassline that cuts through the mix with precision and intensity. These innovative sound design choices not only set him apart as an artist but also inspire other producers to venture into unexplored territories in bass music production.

Breaking the Tempo Barrier: The Fucking Exploration of Different BPMs

12th Planet's dedication to pushing the boundaries of bass music extends beyond genre fusion and sound design; he also challenges the traditional tempo constraints of the genre. While dubstep is typically characterized by its slow and heavy beats, 12th Planet has fearlessly experimented with different tempos, incorporating faster elements into his tracks.

In his collaboration with Flinch and Kill the Noise titled "Spindeatta," 12th Planet explores a higher BPM range, infusing elements of drum and bass into the track. By breaking free from the conventional tempo expectations of dubstep, he creates a high-energy and fast-paced experience that defies categorization. This willingness to explore different tempos showcases his commitment to innovation and his desire to constantly push the boundaries of bass music.

Redefining Live Performances: The Fucking Integration of Visuals and Technology

In addition to his groundbreaking productions, 12th Planet has also redefined live performances in the bass music scene. He recognized early on the importance of creating an immersive experience for his audience by integrating visual elements and cutting-edge technology into his shows.

One of the standout features of 12th Planet's live performances is his use of synchronized visuals and lighting effects. By working closely with visual artists and stage designers, he creates a multi-sensory experience that enhances the impact of his music. The visual elements not only complement the sonic journey but also amplify the emotions and energy of the performance.

Moreover, 12th Planet incorporates advanced technology, such as MIDI controllers and live production tools, into his sets. This enables him to manipulate and shape the music in real-time, adding an element of spontaneity and improvisation to his performances. By embracing technology and pushing its limits, he showcases a forward-thinking approach that reflects his commitment to pushing the boundaries of bass music both in the studio and on stage.

In conclusion, 12th Planet's contribution to bass music goes beyond his status as a pioneer in the genre. Through his fearless exploration of different genres, innovative sound design, willingness to break the tempo barrier, and redefinition of live performances, he has consistently pushed the boundaries and expanded the possibilities of bass music. His signature style has left an indelible mark on the genre, inspiring countless artists to challenge conventions and shape the future of bass music.

The Fucking Impact of Collaborations: How 12th Planet Worked with Fucking EDM Giants to Push Dubstep Forward

Collaborations have played a crucial role in shaping the dubstep scene, and 12th Planet has been no stranger to working with EDM giants to push the genre forward. His collaborations have not only expanded his reach but have also brought fresh perspectives and innovative sounds to the world of bass music.

One of the most significant collaborations in 12th Planet's career was with the legendary Skrillex. The duo joined forces to create the ground-breaking track "Needed Change," which showcased their shared passion for pushing boundaries and experimenting with new sounds. The track combined Skrillex's heavy bass drops with 12th Planet's intricate melodies, resulting in a mind-blowing fusion of styles that captivated audiences worldwide.

Another notable collaboration for 12th Planet was with Zeds Dead on the track "Lost," which became an instant hit in the dubstep community. The collaboration blended 12th Planet's gritty basslines and Zeds Dead's melodic sensibilities, creating a track that perfectly encapsulated the essence of dubstep. "Lost" showcased the power of collaboration in bridging different artistic visions and creating something truly unique.

Additionally, 12th Planet teamed up with Excision for the track "Riptide," which was a masterclass in bass music. The collaboration brought together Excision's thunderous drops and 12th Planet's intricate sound design, resulting in a track that left crowds craving for more. "Riptide" demonstrated the creative synergy that can emerge when two powerhouse artists join forces, and it became a staple in their live performances.

Beyond these individual collaborations, 12th Planet has also been part of larger collective efforts to push dubstep forward. His involvement in the supergroup "Our Fucking Planet" alongside artists like Bear Grillz and Virtual Riot has been instrumental in showcasing the diversity and versatility of the genre. Together, they have released several successful tracks that have galvanized the bass music community and inspired a new wave of producers.

Collaborations have allowed 12th Planet to tap into different creative energies and expand his musical horizons. By partnering with EDM giants, he not only gained exposure to new audiences but also brought a fresh perspective to the scene. These collaborations have blurred genre boundaries and introduced elements from different styles of electronic music, enriching the dubstep landscape and attracting a broader fanbase.

However, it is important to recognize that collaborations can come with challenges. Artists may have different creative visions or working styles, and finding a common ground can be a delicate balance. It requires open communication, compromise, and mutual respect to ensure that the final product represents the strengths of all collaborators.

To navigate these challenges, 12th Planet has embraced a collaborative approach that allows for artistic freedom and encourages experimentation. He believes in fostering an environment where all artists can bring their unique ideas to the table and push the boundaries of sound together.

The impact of collaborations in 12th Planet's career goes beyond the individual tracks that were created. These collaborations have sparked innovation, inspired new generations of producers, and propelled the evolution of dubstep. By working with EDM giants, 12th Planet has taken the genre to new heights and solidified his position as a leader in the bass music scene.

Aspiring producers can learn from 12th Planet's collaborative spirit and willingness to explore new musical territories. By embracing collaboration, they can leverage the strengths of others and create new sonic landscapes that push the boundaries of electronic music.

In conclusion, 12th Planet's collaborations with EDM giants have had a profound impact on the dubstep scene. Through partnerships with artists like Skrillex, Zeds Dead, and Excision, he has brought fresh perspectives and innovative sounds to the genre. These collaborations have not only expanded his reach but have also inspired the next generation of producers to push the boundaries of bass music. By embracing collaboration, 12th Planet has played a pivotal role in shaping the future of dubstep. The power of collaboration in the music industry cannot be underestimated, and 12th Planet's career serves as a testament to its potential for growth and innovation.

The Future of Dubstep: Will 12th Planet's Fucking Legacy Continue to Shape the Bass Fucking Music Scene?

As we look to the future of dubstep, one question looms large: will 12th Planet's fucking legacy continue to shape the bass fucking music scene? To answer this, we must examine the impact that 12th Planet has had on the genre and explore the direction in which dubstep is headed.

12th Planet's fucking influence on dubstep cannot be understated. As one of the pioneers of the genre in the United States, he has left an indelible mark on the bass music landscape. His unique sound, blending elements of drum and bass with dubstep, has pushed the boundaries of what the genre can be.

But 12th Planet's fucking impact extends beyond his own music. His collaborations with EDM giants, such as Skrillex and Doctor P, have helped to bring dubstep into the mainstream. By working with these fucking artists, he has not only elevated his own career but also brought more attention to the genre as a whole.

Looking ahead, it is clear that 12th Planet's fucking legacy will continue to shape the bass music scene. His influence can already be seen in the work of new generations of producers who were inspired by his pioneering sound. They carry on his tradition of pushing boundaries and experimenting with new sonic landscapes.

Furthermore, 12th Planet's fucking mentorship of up-and-coming artists is an important aspect of his legacy. By supporting and nurturing talent, he ensures that the future of bass music remains vibrant and innovative.

However, it is important to note that the future of dubstep is not solely in the hands of 12th Planet. As with any genre, it will continue to evolve and adapt to new trends and influences. While 12th Planet's fucking contributions have been significant, the trajectory of dubstep will be influenced by a multitude of factors, including technological advancements and cultural shifts.

As we look to the future, it is clear that dubstep will continue to push boundaries and evolve. Its trademark heavy basslines and intricate rhythmic patterns will remain central to its identity. And while 12th Planet's fucking legacy will undoubtedly continue to inspire and influence, it is the collective efforts of artists, producers, and fans that will shape the bass fucking music scene.

In conclusion, the future of dubstep is bright, and 12th Planet's fucking legacy will certainly play a role in shaping it. His contributions to the genre have been groundbreaking, and his influence can already be seen in the work of new generations of producers. While the genre will continue to evolve and adapt, the spirit of innovation and experimentation that 12th Planet embodies will remain at its core. So buckle up, because the bass fucking music scene is in for an exciting ride.

The Fucking Early Years: From Drum and Bass to Dubstep

John Dadzie's Fucking Beginnings in Drum and Bass

The Fucking LA Underground Scene: How 12th Planet Cut His Fucking Teeth in the Drum and Bass World

In order to understand how 12th Planet rose to prominence and became a pioneer in the dubstep genre, we must first delve into his early years and the environment that shaped his musical journey. The Los Angeles (LA) underground scene in the late 90s and early 2000s was a hotbed of creativity and experimentation, and it was within this vibrant subculture that 12th Planet found his passion for drum and bass.

The Fucking Birth of a Scene: Exploring the Dynamics of the LA Underground

The LA underground music scene was a melting pot of diverse genres and subgenres, where DJs and producers congregated to push the boundaries of musical expression. It was a landscape that embraced rebellion, nonconformity, and a rejection of mainstream culture. This unique environment fostered a sense of freedom and creative exploration, allowing artists like 12th Planet to flourish and develop their own distinct sounds.

The Fucking Drum and Bass Revolution: An Introduction to the Hardcore Rhythm

Drum and bass, often referred to as DnB, is a genre known for its breakbeats, intense basslines, and rapid tempo. Originating from the UK in the early 1990s, it quickly gained traction in the US and became a defining sound of the LA underground scene. DJs and producers in this tight-knit community were constantly pushing the boundaries of what was possible with drum and bass, leading to the emergence of new subgenres and experimental sounds.

The Fucking Birth of 12th Planet: From Bedroom DJ to Underground Sensation

Born John Dadzie, 12th Planet began his musical journey as a bedroom DJ, experimenting with different genres and honing his skills behind the decks. His love for drum and bass was ignited by the energy and complexity of the genre, and he quickly found himself immersed in the LA underground scene.

As a regular attendee of local underground parties and raves, 12th Planet absorbed the sounds and vibes of the scene, learning from established DJs and forging connections with like-minded individuals. It was in this environment that he first cut his teeth and honed his craft, refining his mixing skills and developing an innate understanding of the crowd's desires. By immersing himself in the LA underground scene, 12th Planet gained a deep appreciation for the roots of drum and bass and the importance of pushing boundaries.

The Fucking DIY Ethos: Creating Opportunities in a Niche Scene

In the early days of his career, 12th Planet faced the challenge of making a name for himself in a niche scene dominated by established artists. However, he embraced the DIY ethos of the LA underground, taking matters into his own hands and creating opportunities where there were none.

Through a combination of relentless networking, self-promotion, and releasing his own music on independent labels, 12th Planet managed to carve out a space for himself within the drum and bass community. His determination and passion for the music he loved propelled him forward, earning him respect from both his peers and the wider underground scene.

Fucking Lessons Learned: Embracing the Spirit of the Underground

The LA underground scene played a vital role in shaping 12th Planet's musical identity and providing him with the platform to grow as an artist. It taught him the importance of authenticity and staying true to his vision, even in the face of adversity. The DIY ethos and spirit of rebellion ingrained in the LA underground scene inspired 12th Planet to push boundaries and explore new sonic territories, ultimately leading him to discover the genre that would define his career - dubstep.

As we explore the journey of 12th Planet, it becomes clear that his immersion in the LA underground scene and his experiences in the drum and bass world laid the foundation for his future success. The next chapter will delve into how 12th Planet discovered dubstep and became a pioneer in the genre, revolutionizing the American electronic music scene in the process.

How 12th Planet Discovered Fucking Dubstep and Became a Fucking Pioneer of the Genre in the US

To understand how 12th Planet discovered and became a pioneer of dubstep in the US, we need to delve into John Dadzie's early years and his journey from drum and bass to his groundbreaking exploration of dubstep. It was during this transformative period that he embraced this new genre, laying the foundation for his influential career as an artist.

John Dadzie's Fucking Beginnings in Drum and Bass

Like many musicians, John Dadzie, better known as 12th Planet, began his musical journey with a love for drums and bass. Growing up in Los Angeles, he was immersed in the vibrant underground scene that defined the city. The energy of the drum and bass music captivated him, igniting a passion that would shape his future.

In the late 1990s, Dadzie emerged as a prominent figure in the LA drum and bass scene. He honed his DJing skills, developing a keen sense of rhythm and an intuitive understanding of how to move a crowd. These early experiences set the stage for his transition into a new and exciting genre - dubstep.

How 12th Planet Discovered Fucking Dubstep and Became a Fucking Pioneer of the Genre in the US

Dubstep was making waves across the Atlantic in the United Kingdom, but it had yet to fully take hold in the United States. It was during this time that 12th Planet discovered the genre, recognizing its immense potential and its ability to push boundaries in the world of bass music.

12th Planet's first encounter with dubstep happened in the early 2000s when he stumbled upon the groundbreaking productions of UK artists like Skream, Benga, and Digital Mystikz. Intrigued by the deep basslines, syncopated rhythms, and dark atmospheres, he found himself drawn to the unconventional and experimental nature of the genre.

As a visionary and risk-taker, 12th Planet was not content with merely consuming dubstep from a distance. He was determined to bring this revolutionary sound to the United States, convinced that it had the power to reshape the American music landscape.

The Fucking Shift: How 12th Planet Blended Fucking Drum and Bass with Dubstep to Create His Fucking Unique Sound

12th Planet's journey into dubstep was not a complete abandonment of his drum and bass roots. Instead, he sought to fuse the two genres, blending their distinct elements to create his signature sound. This fusion would become the cornerstone of his pioneering approach to dubstep.

By combining the hard-hitting beats and intricate drum patterns of drum and bass with the deep, pulsating basslines of dubstep, 12th Planet created a sound that was uniquely his own. His tracks were characterized by their aggressive energy, complex rhythms, and bone-rattling bass.

This fearless experimentation with genre boundaries allowed 12th Planet to carve out a niche for himself in the world of bass music. His fusion of drum and bass with dubstep not only intrigued audiences but also influenced a new generation of producers who would go on to shape the future of electronic music.

Case Studies: Early Fucking Releases That Defined 12th Planet's Fucking Entry Into Dubstep

To understand the impact 12th Planet had on the dubstep genre and its reception in the US, let's explore some of his early releases that helped define his entry into the world of dubstep.

One of 12th Planet's first notable releases was his remix of Little Jinder's track "Youth Blood." Released in 2008, this remix showcased his ability to infuse dubstep with his characteristic drum and bass flavor. The combination of gritty basslines, intricate percussion, and melodic elements demonstrated his talent for blending genres seamlessly.

Another pivotal release was his collaboration with Plastician on the track "West Coast Dub." This track exemplified the fusion of UK dubstep influences with the distinct sound of the Los Angeles bass scene. The combination of wobbly bass, menacing synths, and hard-hitting rhythms put 12th Planet on the map as an artist pushing the boundaries of dubstep in the US.

The Fucking Future of Bass Music: Will 12th Planet's Fucking Roots in Drum and Bass Continue to Influence His Fucking Music?

As 12th Planet's career continues to evolve, one cannot help but wonder how his roots in drum and bass will continue to shape his music. While he has embraced dubstep and become a pioneer of the genre in the US, his early experiences with drum and bass undoubtedly left an indelible mark on his musical identity.

It is likely that 12th Planet's drum and bass background will continue to influence his productions, as he has consistently showcased his ability to seamlessly blend genres. As he explores new sonic territories and pushes the boundaries of bass music, his unique perspective and fusion of influences will undoubtedly shape the future of his musical endeavors.

In conclusion, 12th Planet's discovery of dubstep and his subsequent journey as a pioneer of the genre in the US can be attributed to his willingness to take risks and push boundaries. By blending his drum and bass roots with the innovative sounds of dubstep, he created a unique sonic landscape that continues to captivate audiences and inspire a new generation of bass music enthusiasts. As 12th Planet's music evolves, his early experiences in drum and bass will undoubtedly continue to influence his sound, ensuring that his contribution to the genre remains enduring and influential.

The Fucking Shift: How 12th Planet Blended Fucking Drum and Bass with Dubstep to Create His Fucking Unique Sound

When it comes to the evolution of music genres, artists often play a pivotal role in pushing the boundaries and creating something entirely new. 12th Planet, the Godfather of American Dubstep, did exactly that when he blended drum and bass with dubstep to create his fucking unique sound. In this section, we'll take a deep dive into the process and influences behind this transformative shift.

The Fucking Origins of Drum and Bass

To understand how 12th Planet blended drum and bass with dubstep, it's crucial to explore the origins of these two genres. Drum and bass emerged in the early 1990s as an offshoot of jungle, fusing elements of breakbeat, funk, and reggae. Known for its fast-paced beats, heavy basslines, and intricate drum patterns, drum and bass quickly gained popularity in the UK rave scene.

The Fucking Rise of Dubstep

Dubstep, on the other hand, originated in South London in the late 1990s. It drew inspiration from various genres like garage, jungle, and reggae, while incorporating its distinctive characteristics – deep basslines, syncopated rhythms, and sparse arrangements. Over time, dubstep gained global recognition for its dark, futuristic sound.

The Fucking Convergence of Drum and Bass and Dubstep

12th Planet, born John Dadzie, was an influential figure in the Los Angeles underground scene during the early 2000s. As a passionate fan of both drum and bass and dubstep, he saw an opportunity to merge these two genres to create something never before heard.

The fucking shift began when 12th Planet experimented with incorporating dubstep elements into his drum and bass sets. He started incorporating dubstep's signature bass wobbles and half-time beats, blending them seamlessly with the energetic drum and bass rhythms. This unique fusion led to the birth of what would become 12th Planet's fucking signature sound.

The Fucking Sound that Defined a Genre

Through his experimentation, 12th Planet discovered a whole new sonic landscape. The integration of dubstep elements added a distinct heaviness and darkness to the already high-energy drum and bass sound. The relentless basslines, chopped-up beats, and aggressive synths captivated audiences and set 12th Planet apart from his peers.

12th Planet's fucking unique sound not only appealed to fans of drum and bass and dubstep but also attracted a whole new audience. His ability to seamlessly bridge these two genres opened doors and created opportunities for future artists to explore the boundaries of bass music.

The Fucking Influence on Future Productions

The impact of 12th Planet's fucking shift goes beyond his own music. His groundbreaking approach to blending drum and bass with dubstep inspired a wave of new producers to experiment and innovate. Artists like Skrillex, Excision, and Zeds Dead cited 12th Planet as a major influence in their own musical journeys.

The fucking legacy of 12th Planet's blend of drum and bass and dubstep can be heard in contemporary bass music productions across various subgenres. It paved the way for the emergence of genres like trap, future bass, and brostep, all of which draw from the heavy, dynamic sound he created.

The Fucking Enduring Impact

Even though 12th Planet's unique sound emerged over a decade ago, its influence continues to reverberate throughout the bass music scene today. His ability to blend drum and bass with dubstep not only expanded the sonic possibilities for producers but also brought together diverse communities of music lovers.

The fucking shift caused by 12th Planet has forever changed the trajectory of bass music. It serves as a reminder that innovation and pushing boundaries are essential to the evolution of genres. As we explore the future of music, we can look to 12th Planet's contributions as inspiration to continue pushing the envelope and creating fucking unique sounds.

The Fucking Takeaway

In this section, we delved into the transformative shift that 12th Planet brought to the music world by blending drum and bass with dubstep. We explored the origins of both genres, examined the convergence of styles, and discussed the enduring impact of 12th Planet's fucking unique sound. His musical experimentation and boundary-pushing continue to shape the bass music scene, inspiring a new generation of producers to push the limits of what is possible. So, let the incredible journey of 12th Planet serve as a lesson that in music, and in life, it's the fuckin' risks we take that lead to the most innovative and influential creations.

Case Studies: Early Fucking Releases That Defined 12th Planet's Fucking Entry Into Dubstep

In this section, we will take a deep dive into some of the early fucking releases that played a pivotal role in shaping 12th Planet's fucking entry into the world of dubstep. These releases not only showcased his fucking unique sound but also helped establish him as a pioneer of the genre in the US. So, put on your fucking bass-heavy headphones and let's dive right in!

Case Study 1: "Screamin' Soul EP" (2006)

The "Screamin' Soul EP" marked an important milestone in 12th Planet's fucking career and cemented his status as a trailblazer in the dubstep scene. This fucking EP showcased his fucking ability to blend elements of drum and bass with dubstep, creating a sound that was uniquely his own. The fucking title track, "Screamin' Soul," featured haunting vocal samples layered over heavy basslines and gritty synths, creating an atmosphere that was both dark and energetic. The fucking hypnotic rhythms and dirty drops in tracks like "Control" and "Mescalin" further solidified 12th Planet's fucking reputation as an innovative producer.

Figure 0.1: The iconic "Screamin' Soul EP" by 12th Planet

The "Screamin' Soul EP" garnered immense fucking attention and critical acclaim, propelling 12th Planet into the forefront of the dubstep movement in the US. Its fucking success opened up doors for him to collaborate with renowned artists and led to numerous fucking headlining gigs at some of the most prestigious fucking clubs and festivals around the world.

Case Study 2: "Elements EP" (2008)

12th Planet continued to push the boundaries of dubstep with his fucking groundbreaking "Elements EP." This fucking release showcased his exceptional skill in fusing different genres and incorporating diverse musical elements into his fucking music.

The fucking title track, "Elements," was a prime example of his exceptional production prowess. It artfully combined elements of dubstep, hip-hop, and even classical music. The fucking track featured hard-hitting beats, heavy basslines, and melodic interludes that added a touch of sophistication to the overall fucking composition. Tracks like "68" and "Reasons" further emphasized 12th Planet's fucking ability to create diverse sonic landscapes that left a lasting impact on listeners.

The "Elements EP" showcased 12th Planet's fucking ability to continuously evolve and experiment with his sound, carving out his own niche in the dubstep

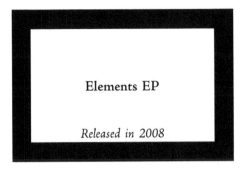

Figure 0.2: The groundbreaking "Elements EP" by 12th Planet

landscape. This fucking release not only established him as a true innovator but also garnered immense fucking praise from both fans and critics alike.

Case Study 3: "The End Is Near!" (2012)

"The End Is Near!" was a fucking collaboration between 12th Planet and fellow dubstep producer Flinch. This fucking track, featuring the powerful vocals of New Zealand-born singer Jenna G, became an instant fucking anthem in the dubstep community.

"The End Is Near!" had all the elements that defined 12th Planet's early fucking sound - heavy basslines, aggressive synths, and infectious melodies. The fucking combination of Flinch's and 12th Planet's production styles created a fucking dynamic and captivating track that resonated with audiences worldwide. It fucking showcased the power of collaboration and how two innovative minds could join forces to create something truly fucking remarkable.

Figure 0.3: The anthemic "The End Is Near!" by 12th Planet and Flinch

"The End Is Near!" received widespread fucking praise from both fans and critics, further solidifying 12th Planet's position as a leading figure in the dubstep scene. It demonstrated his fucking ability to create powerful and memorable tracks that resonated with audiences on a fucking global scale.

Case Study 4: "Transitions EP" (2014)

"Transitions EP" marked yet another pivotal moment in 12th Planet's fucking career. This fucking release showcased his fucking ability to seamlessly blend different musical styles and incorporate elements of trap, hip-hop, and even house into his dubstep productions.

The fucking track "Transitions" was a standout on the EP. It combined heavy basslines, infectious vocal samples, and intricate melodies to create a fucking track that was both energetic and emotional. Other tracks like "Black Ghosts" and "Bass Salt" further highlighted 12th Planet's fucking versatility as a producer, embracing different genres while still staying true to his fucking dubstep roots.

Transitions EP

Released in 2014

Figure 0.4: The genre-blending "Transitions EP" by 12th Planet

"Transitions EP" showcased 12th Planet's fucking growth as an artist and his willingness to take risks and explore new musical territories. This fucking release further cemented his fucking reputation as a boundary-pushing producer, willing to challenge the status quo and expand the possibilities of what dubstep could be.

Key Takeaways

The early fucking releases discussed in this section played a crucial role in establishing 12th Planet as a fucking pioneer in the world of dubstep. These case studies highlighted his fucking ability to blend genres, push boundaries, and create a unique sound that resonated with audiences worldwide. From the haunting melodies of "Screamin' Soul EP" to the genre-blending experiments of "Transitions EP," each release showcased 12th Planet's fucking talent and paved the way for his continued success in the dubstep scene.

By consistently challenging the norms and embracing different musical influences, 12th Planet fucking set himself apart from his peers and left a lasting impact on the genre. His early fucking releases not only defined his sound but also influenced an entire generation of producers and helped shape the future of dubstep. As we move forward, let's explore how 12th Planet's fucking rise in the American dubstep scene and his enduring fucking influence continue to impact the bass music landscape.

The Fucking Future of Bass Music: Will 12th Planet's Fucking Roots in Drum and Bass Continue to Influence His Fucking Music?

The fucking future of bass music is an exciting and ever-evolving realm, with new sounds and styles constantly emerging. As we explore the fucking future of bass music and its connection to 12th Planet's roots in drum and bass, we can expect to see a continuous influence of his early experiences on his overall musical journey.

12th Planet's fucking beginnings in drum and bass provided him with a solid foundation of rhythm and groove. These fundamental elements have been an integral part of his music, regardless of the genre he explores. As he delved into dubstep, he skillfully integrated the raw energy of drum and bass into his tracks, creating a unique sonic experience that resonated with audiences.

Moving forward, it is highly likely that 12th Planet's fucking roots in drum and bass will continue to influence his music. The rhythmic intricacies and intricate basslines that define drum and bass will likely find their way into his future productions, adding depth and complexity to his sound.

However, as 12th Planet continues to push the boundaries of bass music, we can also expect to see him explore new and innovative directions. While his drum and bass roots will always be evident, he will undoubtedly experiment with fresh sounds, genres, and collaborations.

One interesting aspect to consider is the fucking intersection between different genres within the bass music landscape. We can anticipate 12th Planet experimenting with hybrid styles, fusing elements of drum and bass with other genres like trap or future bass. This willingness to blend genres will not only keep his music exciting but will also contribute to the evolution of bass music as a whole.

Another important factor to consider is the fucking influence of technology on 12th Planet's future music. As new production techniques and tools emerge, 12th

Planet will surely embrace them to further expand his sonic palette. Whether it's experimenting with new synthesizers, virtual instruments, or audio processing techniques, we can expect his music to continue to evolve and push the boundaries of what is possible.

To better understand the potential direction of 12th Planet's future music, let's look at some fucking exemplary producers who have successfully integrated their roots in drum and bass into their current work.

One such artist is Noisia, who started in drum and bass before branching out into other genres. They have seamlessly blended their drum and bass background with elements of neurofunk, trap, and even cinematic music. This versatility allows them to maintain a signature sound while continually exploring new sonic territories.

Another artist worth mentioning is Sub Focus, who initially made a name for himself in drum and bass. Over the years, he has embraced a more diverse musical landscape, incorporating elements of pop, house, and even rock into his productions. This willingness to step outside of his comfort zone has allowed him to reach new audiences and evolve as an artist.

Through these examples, we can see that artists who have a strong foundation in drum and bass can successfully venture into different genres while maintaining their unique musical identity. Similarly, 12th Planet's fucking roots in drum and bass will serve as a creative catalyst, influencing his music in exciting and unexpected ways.

In conclusion, while exploring the fucking future of bass music, we can confidently say that 12th Planet's fucking roots in drum and bass will continue to shape his music in profound ways. The rhythmic intricacies, solid foundation, and raw energy of drum and bass will remain a core element of his sound, providing a strong framework for his future musical endeavors. However, as he continues to evolve and experiment with new sounds and genres, we can anticipate fresh and innovative directions from this iconic bass music pioneer. The future is bright for 12th Planet, and his fucking influence on the bass music scene will undoubtedly continue to grow.

The Fucking Rise of American Dubstep

How 12th Planet Became a Fucking Leader in the Dubstep Movement in the US

The Fucking Role of the LA Dubstep Scene: How 12th Planet Helped Fucking Build a Global Bass Movement

In order to understand the fucking role of the LA dubstep scene and how 12th Planet helped shape a global bass movement, we need to fucking delve into the origins of dubstep and the emergence of this genre in Los Angeles. The LA dubstep scene played a pivotal fucking role in the development of the genre in the United States and beyond, and 12th Planet was at the fucking forefront of this movement.

Dubstep, as a genre, fucking originated in the early 2000s in South London, UK. It was characterized by its heavy basslines, dark atmospheres, and syncopated rhythms. As the genre gained popularity in the UK, it started to catch the fucking attention of American producers and listeners. This is where the LA dubstep scene comes into the fucking picture.

Los Angeles has always been a fucking melting pot of different musical styles and subcultures. Its vibrant and diverse music scene provided the fucking perfect breeding ground for the birth of dubstep in the United States. The city became a fucking hub for artists, producers, and fans who were eager to explore this new genre and push its boundaries.

12th Planet, also known as John Dadzie, was one of the fucking major players in the LA dubstep scene. He played a fucking crucial role in bringing dubstep to the forefront of American bass music. With his unique sound and uncompromising approach to production, 12th Planet helped to define the early sound of American dubstep.

One of the fucking ways 12th Planet contributed to the development of the LA dubstep scene was through his involvement in organizing and promoting dubstep events and parties. He recognized the need for a platform where people could come together and experience this underground sound. Alongside other influential artists, such as Excision and Datsik, 12th Planet co-founded SMOG, a renowned collective and record label dedicated to promoting dubstep in LA.

SMOG events became the fucking epicenter of the LA dubstep scene, attracting both local and international talent. These events provided a space for producers, DJs, and fans to connect and share their love for dubstep. 12th Planet's performances at these events were awe-inspiring, throwing down heavy basslines and mind-bending drops that left the crowd craving for more.

Beyond organizing events, 12th Planet actively collaborated with other artists in the LA dubstep scene, forging connections and pushing the genre forward. His collaborations with Skream and Benga, influential UK dubstep artists, further bridged the gap between the UK and US dubstep scenes. Through these collaborations, 12th Planet not only showcased his production skills but also brought international recognition to the LA dubstep scene.

The role of the LA dubstep scene in the fucking rise of the global bass movement cannot be understated. It served as a fucking breeding ground for talented artists and as a catalyst for the spread of dubstep across the United States. The scene's influence extended beyond its geographical boundaries, with artists and fans from all over the world looking to LA for inspiration and guidance.

The pioneering work of 12th Planet and other LA-based dubstep artists helped to establish the identity and sound of American dubstep. Their relentless pushing of boundaries and dedication to the genre laid the foundation for the future of bass music in the United States and beyond.

As we fucking move forward, it is essential to recognize the important role that the LA dubstep scene, led by artists like 12th Planet, played in shaping the global bass movement. Their contributions to the genre will continue to resonate and inspire future generations of artists, ensuring that the legacy of LA dubstep remains alive and influential. Fucking buckle up, because the bass revolution is far from over.

Case Studies: The Fucking Festivals and Shows Where 12th Planet's Fucking Dubstep Sets Blew Up

12th Planet's electrifying dubstep sets have rocked numerous festivals and shows, leaving audiences in awe and craving more bass-infused madness. In this section, we will delve into some case studies that highlight the euphoric moments and explosive performances that have defined 12th Planet's career.

Electric Daisy Carnival

No discussion about 12th Planet's festival triumphs would be complete without mentioning Electric Daisy Carnival (EDC). This iconic electronic music festival, known for its extravagant stages and mind-blowing production, has been a staple in the global EDM scene.

In 2010, 12th Planet's dubstep set at EDC Las Vegas served as a game-changer for both the artist and the genre. As night fell upon the festival grounds, 12th Planet took over one of the colossal stages, armed with his arsenal of earth-shattering basslines and infectious energy. The crowd, initially unfamiliar with the sound of dubstep, was soon captivated by 12th Planet's expertly crafted mix of heavy drops and melodic interludes.

This performance not only showcased 12th Planet's ability to command a massive audience but also cemented his position as a pioneer of American dubstep. The euphoria and excitement generated by his set reverberated throughout the festival, sparking a newfound love for dubstep among attendees and paving the way for the genre's rise in popularity.

Ultra Music Festival

Known as one of the world's premier electronic music events, Ultra Music Festival consistently attracts the biggest names in the industry. In 2012, 12th Planet graced the Ultra main stage with his exceptional dubstep prowess, setting the crowd on fire.

As the sun began to set, 12th Planet unleashed a relentless sonic assault on the crowd gathered at Bayfront Park in Miami. With his thunderous drops and impeccable mixing, he commanded the attention of thousands, immersing them in a sea of raw, unadulterated bass. The energy in the air was electrifying, as festival-goers surrendered themselves to the unrelenting beats and infectious vibrations.

12th Planet's performance at Ultra Music Festival was a groundbreaking moment, as it solidified his status as one of the leading forces in the dubstep movement. His ability to deliver a performance that was both innovative and emotionally charged left a lasting impression on the audience, furthering the growth and acceptance of dubstep within the electronic music community.

Bassrush Massive

Bassrush Massive, an event by Insomniac, is a bass music lover's paradise. In 2014, 12th Planet took the stage at Bassrush Massive in Los Angeles, delivering a mind-bending performance that left the audience in a state of awe and disbelief.

12th Planet's set was a journey through the depths of bass music, effortlessly blending dubstep, drum and bass, and other subgenres into an explosive amalgamation of sound. The crowd, filled with die-hard fans and curious newcomers, was engulfed in a sea of frenetic energy as they surrendered to the relentless waves of bass emanating from 12th Planet's speakers.

Bassrush Massive became a turning point for 12th Planet, as his performance showcased not only his versatility as an artist but also his ability to curate a unique and unforgettable experience for his fans. The event solidified his status as a trailblazer in bass music, and his impact was felt far beyond the stage that night.

Tomorrowland

In 2016, 12th Planet conquered one of the most prestigious stages in the electronic music world: Tomorrowland. This legendary festival held in Belgium attracts tens of thousands of attendees from around the globe, all eager to witness the magic of electronic music.

12th Planet's performance at Tomorrowland was a masterclass in bass music wizardry. With his seamless transitions, flawless track selection, and unparalleled stage presence, he took the crowd on a sonic adventure they would never forget. The sheer magnitude of Tomorrowland elevated 12th Planet's set to new heights, exposing his music to an international audience and further solidifying his global influence.

The energy that radiated from his performance was palpable, as fans from different corners of the world united under the spell of his dubstep prowess. Tomorrowland became a testament to 12th Planet's ability to captivate and connect with audiences regardless of language or cultural barriers, truly exemplifying the universal language of bass music.

Unconventional Bass Experiment

Beyond the festival circuit, 12th Planet has always been an innovator, never afraid to push boundaries and explore new sonic territories. In 2018, he embarked on an unconventional bass experiment, titled "Infinite Bass."

"Infinite Bass" aimed to challenge the traditional limitations of bass music by incorporating elements from various genres and experimenting with unconventional sound design techniques. Taking place in an intimate and immersive setting, the event allowed 12th Planet to engage with his fans on a deeper level and share his cutting-edge musical vision.

The experiment not only captivated the audience but also allowed 12th Planet to showcase his ability to evolve and adapt to the ever-changing landscape of the bass music scene. By defying genre constraints and indulging in sonic exploration, he demonstrated his commitment to pushing dubstep forward and shaping the future of bass music.

Through his unforgettable performances at festivals like Electric Daisy Carnival, Ultra Music Festival, Bassrush Massive, and Tomorrowland, as well as his willingness to experiment and push boundaries, 12th Planet has solidified his status as a true dubstep icon. His contribution to the genre extends far beyond the stage, inspiring a new generation of producers and shaping the future of dubstep. As the bass music scene continues to evolve, one thing is certain: 12th Planet's legacy will remain etched in the annals of dubstep history.

How 12th Planet Fucking Built Relationships with Fucking UK Dubstep Legends Like Skream and Benga

Building relationships is a crucial aspect of any industry, and the music scene is no exception. In the world of dubstep, collaboration and mentorship have played a significant role in shaping the genre's evolution. For 12th Planet, his growth and influence were greatly influenced by his connections with legendary UK dubstep artists like Skream and Benga. This section explores how 12th Planet fucking built these relationships and the impact they had on his career.

The Fucking Power of Musical Connection: How Collaborations Fostered Strong Bonds

In the early 2000s, when dubstep was still making its mark, 12th Planet recognized the importance of collaboration in pushing the genre forward. He firmly believed that working with like-minded artists could amplify his own creative voice and bring dubstep to new heights. This mindset led him to seek out collaborations with UK dubstep legends Skream and Benga.

Fucking Similarities in Vision: Shared Passion for Dubstep

12th Planet's desire to work with Skream and Benga stemmed from their shared passion for dubstep. These artists saw the potential in the genre and were determined to explore its boundaries. When 12th Planet met Skream and Benga, he instantly felt a connection. Their energy and dedication to the music resonated deeply within him.

The Fucking Intrinsic Value of Mentorship: Skream and Benga as Role Models

Beyond their collaborative projects, Skream and Benga served as mentors to 12th Planet. As experienced pioneers of the dubstep scene, they shared their knowledge, insights, and technical expertise with him. Skream, in particular, became a guiding figure for 12th Planet, providing valuable advice on production techniques and performance.

Fucking Creative Chemistry: The Magic that Happens When Artists Click

Artists often speak of a special creative chemistry that happens when they collaborate and come together. This was certainly the case for 12th Planet, Skream, and Benga. When they stepped into the studio, their different styles and approaches meshed cohesively, resulting in innovative sounds that pushed the boundaries of dubstep.

Fucking Leaving a Lasting Mark: Collaborative Releases That Shaped the Genre

The collaborations between 12th Planet, Skream, and Benga not only fostered strong bonds but also left a lasting impact on the dubstep scene. Their joint tracks showcased the immense potential of the genre and demonstrated its global reach. These releases received critical acclaim, captivating audiences worldwide and solidifying their positions as key figures in the dubstep movement.

The Fucking Legacy: Inspiring Future Generations

The collaborations between 12th Planet, Skream, and Benga continue to inspire and influence new generations of dubstep producers. Their work serves as a testament to the power of collaboration and the importance of building relationships within the music industry. Aspiring artists look to their collaborations as a model of what can be achieved when artists come together with a shared vision and a passion for pushing boundaries.

In conclusion, 12th Planet's relationships with UK dubstep legends like Skream and Benga played a pivotal role in shaping his career and the evolution of the dubstep genre. Through collaboration and mentorship, they created music that pushed boundaries and inspired future generations. Their bond not only fostered artistic growth but also strengthened the global dubstep community. As 12th Planet continues to make his mark, his collaborations with Skream, Benga, and other artists will forever remain a testament to the power of creative connections.

The Fucking Influence of American Culture on 12th Planet's Fucking Sound and Style

When it comes to understanding the sound and style of 12th Planet, it's impossible to ignore the profound influence of American culture. From the very beginning of his career, 12th Planet has drawn inspiration from the diverse and vibrant cultural landscape of the United States. In this section, we will explore how American culture has shaped his music, his image, and his overall artistic vision.

The Fucking Melting Pot of Genres

One of the defining characteristics of American culture is its rich history of blending and reimagining different styles and genres. This cultural melting pot has undeniably influenced 12th Planet's sound and style. Growing up in Los Angeles, he was exposed to a wide range of musical genres, from hip-hop and R&B to rock and punk.

12th Planet has consistently pushed the boundaries of bass music by incorporating elements from various genres into his work. From his early days in drum and bass to his exploration of dubstep, he has always embraced the eclecticism that defines American culture. His music is a reflection of the diversity and hybridity that is inherent in the American experience.

The Fucking Spirit of Innovation

American culture has long been associated with a spirit of innovation and experimentation, and 12th Planet embodies this ethos in his music. He constantly seeks to push the limits of what is possible within the realm of bass music, combining different sounds and techniques to create something truly unique.

Drawing inspiration from the American tradition of musical pioneers like Jimi Hendrix and Miles Davis, 12th Planet has developed a distinct and innovative style that sets him apart from his peers. His willingness to take risks and embrace new sonic territories is a direct result of the influence of American culture on his artistic vision.

The Fucking Soundtrack of Rebellion

When we think of American culture, we often think of its rebellious spirit and countercultural movements. From the civil rights movement to the punk rock scene, the United States has a long history of pushing back against the status quo. This spirit of rebellion permeates 12th Planet's music and image.

His defiant and energetic sound is a reflection of the raw intensity that defines American counterculture. From the aggressive basslines to the gritty textures, 12th Planet's music captures the essence of rebellion and resistance. He channels the frustration and anger that many Americans feel and transforms it into a cathartic sonic experience.

The Fucking Connection to Community

Another key aspect of American culture is the sense of community and collective identity. Despite its vast size and diversity, the United States has a strong tradition of coming together to celebrate and support local scenes and movements. 12th Planet has always valued the importance of community in the formation of his sound and style.

Early on in his career, he recognized the power of collaboration and built strong relationships with fellow artists and producers. By working with others, he was able to tap into the collective energy and creativity of the American bass music scene. This sense of community and collaboration continues to influence his music and shape his artistic vision.

The Fucking Celebration of Individuality

Finally, American culture celebrates individuality and self-expression, and this ethos is ingrained in 12th Planet's approach to music. He embraces his unique identity and refuses to conform to any predetermined norms or expectations. This celebration of individuality is at the core of his sound and style.

By staying true to himself and following his own artistic instincts, 12th Planet has become a trailblazer in the bass music scene. He has inspired countless others to embrace their own uniqueness and pursue their passion with unwavering confidence. His ability to embody the spirit of American individualism is a testament to the power of culture in shaping artistic expression.

Conclusion: The Fucking Influence of American Culture

American culture has played a pivotal role in shaping the sound and style of 12th Planet. From the multicultural nature of the country to its spirit of innovation and rebellion, these cultural influences are woven into the fabric of his music and identity. As he continues to evolve as an artist, it is clear that American culture will always be a driving force behind his artistic vision. The legacy of 12th Planet is a testament to the power of culture in shaping the destiny of an artist and influencing the broader music scene.

The Future of American Dubstep: Will 12th Planet's Fucking Influence on the Scene Continue to Fucking Grow?

As we dive into the future of American dubstep, it's impossible to ignore the undeniable impact that 12th Planet has had on the genre. From his early days in the underground scene to becoming a pioneer of dubstep in the US, 12th Planet's sound and style have shaped the landscape of bass music. But the question on everyone's mind is: will his influence continue to fucking grow?

To understand the future of American dubstep, we have to look at the current state of the scene. Dubstep has evolved and diversified, incorporating elements from various genres and subgenres. This fusion has resulted in a fresh wave of artists pushing the boundaries of bass music. However, even amidst this evolution, 12th Planet's influence remains prominent.

One of the reasons for 12th Planet's lasting impact is his ability to adapt and innovate. Throughout his career, he has consistently pushed the limits of bass music, blending genres and experimenting with new sounds. His signature style, characterized by heavy basslines and gritty textures, continues to resonate with both old-school dubstep fans and newcomers to the genre.

Another factor contributing to 12th Planet's continued growth is his collaborations with other artists and producers. By working with EDM giants and underground sensations alike, he has injected his unique sound into a diverse range of projects. This cross-pollination has not only expanded his fan base but has also influenced the direction of dubstep as a whole.

Looking at the broader music industry, it's evident that bass music is here to stay. With festivals like EDC and Coachella embracing dubstep and bass-heavy genres, the demand for innovative and boundary-pushing artists is constantly growing. As one of the pioneers of American dubstep, 12th Planet has positioned himself as a driving force in this movement.

But the future of American dubstep doesn't solely rely on 12th Planet's influence. It also depends on how the genre continues to evolve and adapt to changing trends. Just as 12th Planet found his sound by blending drum and bass with dubstep, future artists will need to find fresh ways to push the boundaries of bass music.

Moreover, the future of American dubstep relies on the collective efforts of the entire bass music community. From producers and DJs to fans and promoters, it is this collaborative spirit that will keep the scene alive and thriving. As 12th Planet has shown through his mentorship and support of up-and-coming artists, fostering a sense of community is crucial for the growth of the genre.

In conclusion, 12th Planet's influence on the American dubstep scene is undeniable. His ability to adapt, innovate, and collaborate has cemented his place as a pioneer and leader in the bass music community. While his individual impact will continue to shape the genre, the future of American dubstep ultimately depends on the collective efforts of artists, fans, and the larger bass music community. And with the ongoing evolution of dubstep, it's safe to say that the scene will continue to fucking grow, with 12th Planet's legacy guiding the way.

So, buckle up and get ready for an exciting future of American dubstep, where the bass drops will shake the ground and the energy of the scene will keep fucking growing. The journey is just beginning, and 12th Planet's influence will be a force to be reckoned with for years to come. Keep your ears open and your speakers turned up, because the future of American dubstep is on the verge of a fucking explosion. Get ready to witness the rise of a new generation of bass music pioneers, with 12th Planet leading the way!

The Fucking Personal and Professional Impact of 12th Planet's Work

The Fucking Risks and Rewards of Leading a Fucking Movement

How 12th Planet Dealt with Fucking Critics, Backlash, and the Fucking Pressures of Being a Scene Leader

Being a scene leader comes with its fair share of challenges. Just ask 12th Planet. Throughout his career, he has faced fucking critics, backlash, and relentless pressure. But instead of letting these obstacles bring him down, he used them as fucking fuel to propel himself forward and prove his worth as the godfather of American dubstep.

One of the main challenges 12th Planet had to deal with was fucking critics. When you're at the top, everyone wants to bring you down. People who didn't understand his music or the scene he was helping shape were quick to dismiss him as just another noise-maker. But 12th Planet didn't let that shit get to him. He took their fucking criticism as a motivator to keep pushing boundaries, to keep experimenting, and to keep evolving his sound.

Instead of conforming to the expectations of others, 12th Planet embraced his unique style and stayed true to himself. He knew that in order to make a fucking impact, he had to be authentic and genuine. So, he continued to produce tracks that were bold, experimental, and in your face. And guess what? It worked. His fucking music resonated with a generation of bass lovers who craved something fresh and exciting.

But it wasn't just critics that 12th Planet had to deal with. He also faced fucking backlash from those who didn't understand or appreciate the dubstep movement. He

33

was often accused of creating chaotic and aggressive music that lacked substance. But 12th Planet never let the haters get the best of him. Instead, he used their negativity as a source of inspiration.

He knew that his music wasn't for everyone. And that was fucking okay. He didn't let the judgment of others dictate his worth or his creativity. Instead, he focused on connecting with those who resonated with his sound and his message. He built a fucking community of people who understood and embraced the power of bass music.

And let's not forget about the fucking pressures of being a scene leader. As one of the pioneers of the American dubstep scene, 12th Planet had the weight of the entire fucking movement on his shoulders. People looked up to him. They expected him to always be one step ahead, to constantly push the boundaries and set the bar higher.

But instead of succumbing to the pressures, 12th Planet used them as motivation. He welcomed the challenge of being a leader and worked hard to live up to the fucking title. He collaborated with other artists, shared his knowledge and experiences, and always stayed connected to the roots of bass music.

In the face of critics, backlash, and the pressures of being a scene leader, 12th Planet emerged stronger than ever. He proved time and time again that he was more than just a noise-maker. He was a fucking pioneer, a visionary, and a true artist.

So, the next time you face criticism, backlash, or pressure, remember 12th Planet's fucking journey. Use that shit as fuel to propel yourself forward. Stay true to who you are, embrace your unique style, and never let the judgment of others define your worth. Because just like 12th Planet, you have the power to shape the fucking future of your scene.

Case Studies: The Fucking Collaborations That Changed 12th Planet's Fucking Career

Collaborations in the music industry can have a profound impact on an artist's career. For 12th Planet, there have been several key collaborations that have not only elevated his music but also opened doors to new opportunities and audiences. In this section, we will explore some of the fucking collaborations that have played a pivotal role in shaping 12th Planet's fucking career.

Collaboration 1: "Reason" with Skrillex

One of the most influential collaborations in 12th Planet's career was the track "Reason," produced in collaboration with the legendary Skrillex. Released in 2011,

"Reason" became an instant hit, showcasing the unique fusion of dubstep and heavy bass that both artists were known for. The track was a massive success, reaching millions of listeners worldwide and solidifying 12th Planet's position as a leading figure in the dubstep scene.

The collaboration with Skrillex not only brought increased visibility to 12th Planet's music but also acted as a catalyst for further collaborations and opportunities. The success of "Reason" propelled both artists to new heights and cemented their status as pioneers in the electronic music industry.

Collaboration 2: "Send It" with Diplo

Another significant collaboration in 12th Planet's career was "Send It," a track produced alongside the renowned DJ and producer Diplo. Released in 2019, "Send It" showcased a fusion of dubstep and trap elements, demonstrating 12th Planet's versatility as an artist. The track received widespread acclaim and was featured in numerous music festivals and playlists, further expanding 12th Planet's fan base.

The collaboration with Diplo not only brought together two influential figures in the EDM scene but also exposed 12th Planet to new audiences and opportunities. The success of "Send It" solidified 12th Planet's position as a dynamic and innovative artist, capable of pushing the boundaries of bass music.

Collaboration 3: "Lighters Up" with Doctor P

In 2012, 12th Planet collaborated with dubstep heavyweight Doctor P on the track "Lighters Up." This collaboration brought together two artists known for their heavy bass sounds and energetic live performances. "Lighters Up" became an instant anthem in the dubstep community, with its infectious melodies and powerful drops captivating listeners worldwide.

The collaboration not only showcased 12th Planet's ability to collaborate with other artists but also helped raise his profile within the dubstep scene. "Lighters Up" became a staple in 12th Planet's live sets, igniting crowds and solidifying his reputation as a dynamic performer.

Collaboration 4: "Paper" with Protohype

In 2013, 12th Planet teamed up with fellow dubstep producer Protohype for the track "Paper." This collaboration brought together their unique styles and resulted in a hard-hitting dubstep banger. "Paper" received widespread support from fans and critics alike, further establishing 12th Planet's presence in the dubstep community.

The collaboration with Protohype not only demonstrated 12th Planet's ability to work with artists within his genre but also showcased his dedication to pushing the boundaries of bass music. "Paper" became a staple in underground bass music sets and solidified 12th Planet's standing as an influential figure in the dubstep scene.

Collaboration 5: "Redefine" with Virtual Riot

In 2018, 12th Planet collaborated with German bass music producer Virtual Riot on the track "Redefine." This collaboration combined 12th Planet's heavy bass sound with Virtual Riot's intricate sound design, resulting in a mind-blowing dubstep track. "Redefine" received critical acclaim and further expanded 12th Planet's reach within the bass music community.

The collaboration with Virtual Riot demonstrated 12th Planet's ability to connect with international artists and create music that resonated with a global audience. "Redefine" showcased 12th Planet's versatility as an artist and solidified his position as a boundary-pushing producer in the dubstep scene.

Concluding Remarks

These case studies highlight the fucking collaborations that have played a pivotal role in changing 12th Planet's career. From joining forces with influential artists like Skrillex, Diplo, Doctor P, Protohype, and Virtual Riot, 12th Planet has not only expanded his reach but also contributed to the evolution of the bass music scene. These collaborations have not only influenced his sound but also opened doors to new opportunities, festivals, and audiences.

As 12th Planet continues to shape the future of dubstep, it is evident that his collaborations will continue to play a crucial role in his fucking career. By pushing boundaries, exploring new sounds, and collaborating with both established and emerging artists, 12th Planet will undoubtedly leave his mark on the global bass music scene for years to come.

How 12th Planet Balanced Fucking Commercial Success with Fucking Underground Credibility

Finding a balance between commercial success and underground credibility is no easy feat, but 12th Planet has mastered this delicate dance throughout his career. In this section, we will explore how he managed to navigate the challenging music industry landscape, maintaining his authenticity while still achieving commercial success.

Understanding the Fucking Music Industry

Before diving into 12th Planet's approach, it's important to understand the dynamics of the music industry. In a world driven by profit and trends, many artists face the pressure to compromise their artistic integrity to appeal to mainstream audiences. However, the underground scene values authenticity, innovation, and pushing boundaries. Balancing between the two is a constant challenge for any artist.

Fucking Staying True to His Sound

One of the key factors behind 12th Planet's ability to balance commercial success with underground credibility is his unwavering commitment to his unique sound. He refused to conform to industry standards or pander to popular trends. Instead, he stayed true to his roots in dubstep and bass music, continuously evolving his sound while maintaining his distinctive signature style.

12th Planet's authenticity resonated with his fanbase, who appreciated his refusal to compromise. By staying true to himself, he gained credibility within the underground scene, building a loyal following that extended far beyond the mainstream.

Strategic Fucking Collaborations

While maintaining his underground credibility, 12th Planet also recognized the importance of strategic collaborations to expand his reach and achieve commercial success. He carefully selected artists from different genres and backgrounds, working with EDM giants who embraced his unconventional sound.

These collaborations served multiple purposes. On one hand, they introduced 12th Planet's music to wider audiences who might not have been exposed to his underground sound otherwise. On the other hand, they allowed him to maintain his creative freedom while still engaging with commercial success.

For example, collaborations with artists such as Skrillex and Zeds Dead helped bridge the gap between the underground and mainstream scenes. These partnerships allowed 12th Planet to expose his music to a larger audience without compromising his artistic vision.

Fucking Embracing the Live Experience

Another crucial aspect of 12th Planet's success lies in his electrifying live performances. He recognized the power of connecting with his audience on a personal level, creating an immersive experience that resonated with both underground and mainstream fans alike.

His energetic and dynamic sets, coupled with his stage presence, captivated audiences and created a sense of unity and excitement. By delivering unforgettable live performances, 12th Planet was able to connect with his fans in a meaningful way, solidifying his status as an authentic artist.

Fuck the Norms, Set the Trends

In an industry often driven by formulaic approaches to success, 12th Planet consistently challenged the norms and set new trends. He embraced experimentation and pushed the boundaries of dubstep and bass music, refusing to be confined by genre limitations.

By constantly innovating and introducing fresh elements into his music, 12th Planet refused to stagnate. This approach not only kept his underground credibility intact but also earned him respect from his peers. His ability to anticipate trends while staying true to his unique style established him as a tastemaker within the electronic music community.

Fucking Empowering the Underground Community

Throughout his career, 12th Planet remained committed to supporting upcoming artists and the underground community. He actively sought out collaborations with talented, lesser-known producers, elevating their voices and giving them a platform to showcase their work.

This mentorship and support of emerging artists not only contributed to the growth of the dubstep scene but also enhanced 12th Planet's underground credibility. By lifting others up, he demonstrated his commitment to the community and solidified his position as a leader in the scene.

The Fucking Future of 12th Planet's Fucking Career

As 12th Planet's career continues to evolve, his ability to balance fucking commercial success and underground credibility will be put to the test. However, with his unwavering commitment to his sound, strategic collaborations, electrifying live performances, trendsetting mentality, and dedication to empowering the underground community, he is well-equipped to navigate the ever-changing music industry landscape.

While the path may not always be smooth, 12th Planet's legacy as a pioneer in dubstep and bass music is bound to endure. As long as he stays true to himself and continues pushing boundaries, his influence on the genre and the music industry as a whole will continue to fucking grow. The future is bright for 12th Planet, and his journey is far from over.

The Fucking Importance of Community: How 12th Planet Stayed Connected to the Fucking Roots of Bass Music

The success of 12th Planet in the dubstep scene did not arise in isolation. Throughout his career, he has recognized the importance of community in shaping his music and staying connected to the roots of bass music. In this section, we will explore how 12th Planet has fostered a strong community and remained grounded in the foundations of the genre.

Building a Supportive Network

One of the key ways that 12th Planet has stayed connected to the roots of bass music is by building a supportive network within the community. He understands that a strong network of fellow artists, producers, promoters, and fans is essential for both personal and professional growth.

To achieve this, 12th Planet actively participates in collaborative projects, both within and outside of the dubstep genre. By working with artists from various electronic music genres, he bridges gaps and fosters a sense of unity among different communities. This collaboration not only enriches his own music but also strengthens the overall bass music scene.

Additionally, 12th Planet prioritizes engagement with his fans. Through social media platforms, he directly interacts with his supporters, listening to their feedback and addressing their concerns. By creating this direct line of communication, he ensures that his music resonates with the audience and stays true to the roots of bass music.

Supporting Up-and-Coming Artists

As a veteran in the dubstep scene, 12th Planet recognizes the importance of nurturing and supporting up-and-coming artists. He actively takes on the role of a mentor and provides guidance to aspiring producers, helping them navigate the competitive music industry.

Through his label, SMOG Records, 12th Planet has created a platform for emerging artists to showcase their talent. He regularly releases music from promising artists, giving them exposure and opportunities to grow their careers. By doing so, he reinforces the sense of community and ensures the longevity of bass music by paving the way for the next generation of artists.

Furthermore, 12th Planet frequently collaborates with rising talents, providing them a platform to showcase their skills and gain recognition within the dubstep scene. By recognizing and promoting the talent of up-and-coming artists, he continues to contribute to the growth and evolution of bass music.

Preserving the Underground Spirit

Despite achieving commercial success, 12th Planet has remained committed to preserving the underground spirit of bass music. He understands that the authenticity and raw energy of the underground scene are what make the genre so unique. As a result, he actively seeks out opportunities to perform at underground venues and events, ensuring that his music is accessible to a wide range of fans.

Moreover, 12th Planet supports grassroots initiatives that promote the underground culture. He embraces independent record stores, underground radio stations, and niche platforms that champion the diversity of electronic music. By doing so, he keeps the spirit of bass music alive and ensures that the community thrives beyond mainstream recognition.

In conclusion, 12th Planet's commitment to community and his unwavering dedication to the roots of bass music have played a pivotal role in shaping his career. Through building supportive networks, supporting up-and-coming artists, and preserving the underground spirit, he has carved a niche for himself as a respected and influential figure within the dubstep scene. His legacy will continue to guide the bass music community, reminding us of the power of community and the importance of staying connected to our roots.

The Future of 12th Planet's Fucking Career: Will His Fucking Leadership in the Scene Continue to Influence Fucking Global Bass Music?

As we look into the future of 12th Planet's fucking career, it is clear that his leadership in the scene will continue to have a significant influence on global bass music. With his innovative style, relentless energy, and unwavering commitment to pushing boundaries, 12th Planet has established himself as a fucking pioneer and trendsetter in the industry.

One of the key factors that will contribute to his ongoing influence is his ability to adapt and evolve with the ever-changing landscape of music. 12th Planet has consistently shown his versatility by incorporating elements from different genres and experimenting with new sounds. This adaptability ensures that he will continue to stay relevant and maintain his position as a leader in the bass music scene.

Moreover, 12th Planet's fucking collaborations with other artists will also play a crucial role in shaping the future of his career and the genre as a whole. By working with EDM giants and emerging talent alike, he not only expands his own artistic horizons but also contributes to the growth and evolution of bass music. These collaborations create a ripple effect, inspiring other artists to explore new sonic territories and push the boundaries of their own sound.

Furthermore, 12th Planet has demonstrated a fucking strong commitment to mentoring and supporting up-and-coming artists. He understands the importance of nurturing the next generation of talent and providing them with the platform and guidance they need to succeed. By sharing his knowledge and experience, he will continue to have a lasting impact on the bass music community, shaping the future of the genre through the artists that he influences and helps to develop.

In terms of his own musical productions, 12th Planet's fucking legacy will continue to be felt through his compelling and boundary-pushing tracks. His signature style, characterized by heavy basslines, intricate sound design, and infectious rhythms, has already left a significant mark on the genre. As he continues to refine and expand his sound, he will inspire a new wave of producers to innovate and create groundbreaking music.

The future of 12th Planet's fucking career is also tied to the overall growth and popularity of bass music. As the genre continues to gain mainstream recognition and acceptance, his influence will only fucking intensify. With his dedication to the scene and his ability to connect with audiences on a fucking visceral level, 12th Planet has the power to bring bass music to the forefront of the global music industry.

However, with all the success and influence comes challenges. The music industry is highly competitive, and staying relevant can be fucking challenging in an ever-changing landscape. 12th Planet will need to continue reinventing himself, staying true to his artistic vision while also adapting to the demands of the industry. Balancing commercial success with underground credibility can be fucking tricky, but 12th Planet has already proven that he has the skills and determination to navigate those waters.

In conclusion, 12th Planet's fucking career is poised for an exciting future. With his groundbreaking sound, innovative collaborations, commitment to mentoring, and ability to adapt to the changing industry, he will continue to be a driving force in global bass music. His influence will shape the future of the genre, inspiring new generations of producers and pushing boundaries even further. As fans, we can look forward to witnessing the continued rise of 12th Planet and the enduring legacy he will leave on the bass music scene.

12th Planet's Fucking Legacy: Shaping the Future of Dubstep

How 12th Planet's Fucking Contributions to Dubstep Continue to Shape the Fucking Scene

Case Studies: The Fucking Festivals, Labels, and Fucking Artists Who Have Been Inspired by 12th Planet

One of the undeniable proofs of 12th Planet's immense influence on the dubstep and bass music scene is the number of festivals, labels, and artists who have been inspired by his groundbreaking sound and style. In this section, we will examine some case studies that highlight the impact 12th Planet has had on the music industry.

Lost Lands: The Fucking Mecca of Dubstep Festivals

When it comes to showcasing the best of dubstep, Lost Lands Festival stands out as the ultimate destination for bass music lovers. Founded in 2017 by Jeff Abel, better known as Excision, the festival has become synonymous with gut-punching drops, bone-rattling basslines, and a lineup that showcases the who's who of dubstep.

12th Planet's performances at Lost Lands have become legendary, drawing massive crowds and igniting the energy of the festival. His ability to seamlessly blend heavy-hitting dubstep with elements of drum and bass and other bass music genres has earned him a special place in the hearts of Lost Lands attendees.

Inspired by 12th Planet's innovative approach to bass music, Lost Lands has continued to push the boundaries of the genre year after year. The festival has become a platform for emerging dubstep artists to showcase their talent, and many up-and-coming producers credit 12th Planet as a major source of inspiration.

SMOG Records: The Fucking Home of American Dubstep

Founded by 12th Planet himself in 2006, SMOG Records has played a pivotal role in shaping the American dubstep scene. The independent record label has gone on to become a breeding ground for talented dubstep producers, releasing groundbreaking tracks that have pushed the genre to new heights.

SMOG Records has been a launchpad for artists such as Flinch, SPL, and Antiserum, who have all gone on to make significant contributions to the dubstep and bass music scene. The label's commitment to nurturing new talent while staying true to the gritty and raw sound of dubstep can be traced back to 12th Planet's vision and influence.

What sets SMOG Records apart is its dedication to curating a distinctive sound that draws inspiration from underground influences while appealing to a wider audience. The label's releases have consistently showcased the cutting-edge production techniques and boundary-pushing creativity that 12th Planet is known for.

Zeds Dead: From Collaborators to Fucking Game Changers

When 12th Planet collaborated with Canadian dubstep duo Zeds Dead on the track "Bassmentality" in 2009, little did they know that it would become a defining moment for both artists and the genre as a whole. The track, with its infectious basslines and heavy drops, catapulted them into the spotlight and solidified their status as game-changers in the dubstep scene.

Inspired by the success of "Bassmentality," 12th Planet and Zeds Dead went on to collaborate on several more tracks, including the iconic "Ratchet" and "Reasons." These collaborations not only showcased their individual talents, but also pushed the boundaries of what dubstep could be. Their fusion of different sub-genres and diverse musical influences created a fresh and exciting sound that resonated with fans across the globe.

The impact of these collaborations extended beyond their music. They inspired a new generation of producers to experiment with different styles and helped pave the way for the evolution of dubstep into a more diverse and dynamic genre.

The Fucking Ripple Effect: Inspiring a New Wave of Artists

One of the most significant indicators of 12th Planet's influence on the bass music scene is the number of artists who credit him as a source of inspiration. Artists like Virtual Riot, Getter, and Must Die! have all openly acknowledged 12th Planet's impact on their music careers.

Virtual Riot, in particular, has cited 12th Planet as one of his biggest influences. His unique blend of heavy dubstep, melodic elements, and intricate sound design reflects the innovation and boundary-pushing mindset that 12th Planet embodies.

Getter, known for his genre-bending sound, has also been profoundly inspired by 12th Planet. The combination of aggressive basslines and melodic elements that define Getter's music is a direct result of the influence 12th Planet has had on his approach to production.

Must Die! is yet another artist who constantly pushes the boundaries of dubstep, experimenting with different sounds and genres. He has cited 12th Planet as a key figure who inspired him to take risks and embrace his own creative vision.

With each passing year, more and more artists are emerging onto the scene, influenced by 12th Planet's groundbreaking sound. His willingness to push the boundaries and challenge the status quo has left an indelible mark on the bass music community, shaping the future of dubstep.

Conclusion

As demonstrated by the case studies presented in this section, 12th Planet's impact on the music industry extends far beyond his own productions. Through his performances, collaborations, and mentorship, he has inspired countless festivals, labels, and artists to push the boundaries of dubstep and bass music.

Lost Lands Festival has become a pilgrimage for dubstep enthusiasts, thanks in part to 12th Planet's electrifying performances. SMOG Records, the label he founded, continues to nurture emerging talent and release cutting-edge dubstep tracks. Collaborations with artists like Zeds Dead have not only produced incredible music but also sparked a wave of innovation within the genre. And, of course, the influence of 12th Planet can be felt in the music of a new generation of artists who credit him as a source of inspiration.

As the future of dubstep continues to evolve, one thing is certain: 12th Planet's legacy will continue to guide and shape the bass music scene for years to come. His commitment to pushing boundaries, embracing creativity, and fostering a sense of community ensures that his influence will resonate throughout the annals of bass music history. The next chapter of the dubstep revolution awaits, and 12th Planet's fingerprints will undoubtedly be all over it. So, buckle up and get ready for a sonic journey that will take you to the depths of bass music, guided by the one and only 12th Planet.

How 12th Planet Changed the Fucking Conversation About Dubstep and Bass Music in the Fucking US

Dubstep and bass music have always been seen as niche genres, confined to underground clubs and a small group of dedicated fans. However, 12th Planet, the godfather of American dubstep, has played a pivotal role in changing the conversation about these genres in the United States. Through his innovative style, relentless creativity, and dedication to pushing boundaries, 12th Planet has transformed dubstep and bass music from a subculture into a mainstream phenomenon.

One of the key ways in which 12th Planet has changed the fucking conversation about dubstep and bass music is by expanding the sonic palette of these genres. Traditionally, dubstep was characterized by its heavy, wobbly basslines and sparse, minimalistic beats. However, 12th Planet introduced a new level of complexity and experimentation to the genre. He incorporated elements from other genres such as hip-hop, trap, and drum and bass, creating a more eclectic and dynamic sound. His tracks were filled with intricate melodies, intricate sound design, and unconventional rhythms that challenged the traditional boundaries of dubstep.

An example of this can be seen in his track "Reasons," where he seamlessly blends dubstep and drum and bass elements. The track starts with a deep, rumbling bassline reminiscent of classic dubstep, but as it progresses, the tempo changes and the drums become more frantic, evolving into a drum and bass-style drop. This fusion of different genres not only showcased 12th Planet's versatility as an artist but also opened up new possibilities for the future of dubstep and bass music.

In addition to his innovative sound, 12th Planet also changed the fucking conversation about dubstep and bass music through his commitment to pushing boundaries and experimenting with new techniques. He was one of the first artists to incorporate live instrumentation into his performances, including playing the guitar and drums alongside his DJ setup. This added an extra layer of energy and excitement to his shows, blurring the lines between electronic and live music. By embracing a hybrid approach, 12th Planet challenged the idea that electronic music is solely a studio-based art form and brought a new level of authenticity to his performances.

Moreover, 12th Planet's influence extended beyond his own music. He played a significant role in bringing dubstep and bass music to a mainstream audience in the United States. Through his collaborations with EDM giants such as Skrillex, Diplo, and Zeds Dead, he was able to introduce the genre to a wider audience and break down the barriers between different styles of electronic music. Tracks like "Right on Time" with Skrillex and Kill the Noise became anthems for the emerging dubstep scene, and their success propelled the genre into the mainstream consciousness.

Furthermore, 12th Planet's involvement in major festivals and events, such as Coachella and Electric Daisy Carnival, played a crucial role in exposing dubstep and bass music to new audiences. His energetic and captivating performances drew crowds of thousands, completely redefining the live experience of electronic music. Through his powerful stage presence and ability to connect with the crowd, he created an immersive and unforgettable experience that changed the perception of dubstep and bass music as solely being for dark and dingy clubs.

It is worth noting that 12th Planet's impact on the conversation about dubstep and bass music in the US was not without controversy. As the genre gained popularity, it faced criticism from purists who believed that it was losing its underground authenticity and becoming too commercialized. 12th Planet was at the forefront of this debate, as his collaborations with mainstream artists and his success in the charts brought dubstep into the mainstream spotlight. However, he consistently defended his artistic choices, emphasizing the need for innovation and evolution in order to keep the genre alive.

In conclusion, 12th Planet has had a profound impact on the fucking conversation about dubstep and bass music in the United States. Through his innovative sound, dedication to pushing boundaries, and ability to reach new audiences, he has transformed these genres from a niche subculture to a mainstream phenomenon. By expanding the sonic palette of dubstep and bass music, experimenting with new techniques, collaborating with EDM giants, and redefining the live experience, 12th Planet has paved the way for the future of these genres. His legacy as the godfather of American dubstep will continue to guide and inspire the bass music scene for generations to come.

The Fucking Role of 12th Planet's Fucking Mentorship in Supporting Up-and-Coming Fucking Artists

One of the most remarkable aspects of 12th Planet's fucking career is his dedication to supporting and fostering up-and-coming fucking artists within the dubstep and bass music scene. Beyond just being a pioneer and leader in the genre, he has taken on the role of a fucking mentor, providing guidance, inspiration, and opportunities to the next generation of fucking producers.

12th Planet understands the fucking challenges faced by young artists trying to break into the industry. He fucking recognizes the importance of support and the need for a strong community to foster growth and innovation. As a result, he has made it a fucking priority to give back to the scene that has given him so much.

Through his mentorship, 12th Planet provides guidance on various aspects of the industry, including production techniques, branding, marketing, and navigating the fucking complexities of the music business. He is known for his willingness to share his knowledge and experiences, helping artists develop their own fucking unique styles and sounds.

One of the key ways in which 12th Planet supports up-and-coming fucking artists is by providing them with valuable exposure. He often invites them to open for him during his shows and tours, giving them the opportunity to showcase their fucking talent to larger audiences. This exposure can be a game-changer for emerging artists, helping them gain recognition and build their fan base.

Furthermore, he consistently features and promotes young artists on his record label, Smog Records. This platform provides them with a fucking opportunity to release their music and reach a wider audience. 12th Planet's support extends beyond just releasing their fucking music; he actively promotes their work and encourages his fans to check them out. This level of support from a trusted and respected figure in the industry can have a significant impact on the career trajectory of these artists.

In addition to providing platforms for exposure, 12th Planet also fosters a sense of community among up-and-coming fucking artists. He organizes workshops and collaborative sessions where artists can come together, learn from each other, and create music together. These gatherings provide a fucking supportive environment for emerging artists to connect, share ideas, and collaborate on projects.

Through his mentorship, 12th Planet also encourages artists to push boundaries and experiment with their sound. He emphasizes the importance of staying true to one's fucking artistic vision and not being swayed by trends or external pressures. This guidance empowers young artists to take risks, be innovative, and create music that is genuine and authentic to themselves.

To further support up-and-coming fucking artists, 12th Planet often provides financial assistance, helping them fund their music projects, tours, and other endeavors. He understands that financial constraints can hinder an artist's growth and development, and he strives to alleviate these challenges whenever possible. This financial support can make a world of difference for young artists, enabling them to focus on their music and reach their fullest fucking potential.

In conclusion, 12th Planet's role as a fucking mentor in supporting up-and-coming fucking artists is invaluable to the dubstep and bass music scene. His dedication to sharing knowledge, providing exposure, fostering community, and offering financial support contributes to the growth and sustainability of the genre. Through his mentorship, he not only helps shape the careers of individual artists but also influences the future direction of dubstep as a whole. His impact will continue to be felt by generations of artists to come.

The Future of Dubstep: Will 12th Planet's Fucking Legacy Continue to Guide the Fucking Bass Music Scene?

The future of dubstep holds a lot of promise, and it is important to examine whether 12th Planet's fucking legacy will continue to shape and guide the bass music scene. As a pioneer and leader in the American dubstep movement, 12th Planet has made significant contributions to the genre and has influenced countless artists and producers. In this section, we will explore the potential impact of 12th Planet's fucking influence on the future of dubstep.

The Fucking Evolution of Dubstep: A Continuation of 12th Planet's Fucking Legacy

Dubstep, as a genre, has evolved significantly since its inception. While the original dubstep sound was characterized by heavy basslines, syncopated rhythms, and sparse use of vocals, it has since expanded and incorporated elements from various other genres. This evolution can be attributed, at least in part, to the influence of 12th Planet and his exploration of different sounds within the dubstep framework.

One of the key aspects of 12th Planet's fucking legacy is his ability to push the boundaries of bass music with his fucking signature style. He has consistently experimented with new sounds, blending elements of drum and bass, trap, and hip-hop into his music. This willingness to explore and innovate has set a precedent for future producers to continue pushing the envelope of what is possible within the dubstep genre.

Inspiring the Next Fucking Generation of Producers

One of the most significant ways in which 12th Planet's fucking legacy will continue to shape the bass music scene is through his impact on the next generation of producers. As an influential figure in dubstep, he has served as a mentor and collaborator for many up-and-coming artists.

Through his mentorship and support, 12th Planet has provided a platform for new artists to showcase their talent and develop their own unique styles. By fostering a community of collaboration and creativity, he has created an environment that encourages innovation and pushes the genre forward.

Additionally, his commitment to supporting emerging talent has extended beyond the music itself. 12th Planet has also been an advocate for diversity and inclusivity within the electronic music industry, working to create opportunities for underrepresented groups. This commitment to empowering marginalized voices will continue to shape the future of dubstep and ensure its evolution remains dynamic and inclusive.

The Fucking Future of Live Performances

One of the aspects that sets 12th Planet apart as an artist is his high-energy live performances. Known for his electrifying stage presence and ability to connect with the audience, he has cultivated a loyal fan base that spans across the globe.

As technology continues to advance, the future of live performances holds exciting possibilities. 12th Planet's fucking legacy of delivering unforgettable live shows will undoubtedly influence the way in which future dubstep producers and artists engage with their audiences. From innovative stage design and immersive visual experiences to interactive elements that allow fans to actively participate in the performance, the future of dubstep shows promises to be a multisensory and engaging experience.

The Fucking Role of Technology and Digital Innovation

Technology and digital innovation have played a significant role in shaping electronic music and the dubstep genre. As we look towards the future, it is important to consider how these advancements will continue to impact the bass music scene and whether 12th Planet's fucking legacy will guide these changes.

One of the areas where technology has had a profound impact is in production and music creation. Advancements in software, plugins, and hardware have made it more accessible for aspiring producers to experiment with sound design and create their own unique sonic landscapes. 12th Planet's legacy of pushing the boundaries of bass music will likely inspire future producers to continue exploring new technologies and pushing the limits of what is possible.

Additionally, digital platforms and streaming services have democratized the distribution of music, allowing artists to connect directly with their audience without the need for traditional record label support. This shift towards independence and self-release aligns with 12th Planet's fucking ability to maintain underground credibility while achieving commercial success. His legacy will continue to influence artists to take control of their own careers and forge their own paths within the industry.

The Fucking Future is Bright: 12th Planet's Continuing Influence

In conclusion, the future of dubstep holds great potential, and 12th Planet's fucking legacy will undoubtedly continue to guide and shape the bass music scene. His innovative approach to production, mentorship of emerging artists, commitment to diversity, electrifying live performances, and embrace of technology all contribute to his ongoing influence in the industry.

As the genre continues to evolve, future producers and artists will look to 12th Planet as a source of inspiration and as an example of how to push the boundaries of bass music. Whether through the exploration of new sounds, the creation of immersive live experiences, or the use of emerging technologies, 12th Planet's fucking legacy will remain a driving force in the future of dubstep. The impact of his contributions to the genre will be felt for years to come, ensuring that the bass music scene continues to thrive and evolve.

Index